PARDON MY SILENCE

by
Greg Buffington

CONTENTS

PARDON MY SILENCE

I did not call today, yesterday, or the day before.
I attempted email, but from within me communication
would not prevail,
so, pardon my silence.

I experienced an event, and I needed to vent,
but with you my words and emotions would not be
spent,
so, pardon my silence.

I did not want to share with you my accounts of
death, tragedy, and violence,
so, pardon my silence.

I knew your heart was in despair,
but no form of communication I could bear,
all is not well, war is hell,
so, pardon my silence.

I want my words to be upbeat and sweet,
not a tone of defeat, the aftermath of battle I hold
discreet,
so, pardon my silence.

In spite of my plight, I want your heart to be light,
I'm the one that was sent to fight,
so, pardon my silence.

MAGIC RAIN

One day it started to rain, everyone else took cover and ran inside, my body and soul I did not hide. I sensed it was magic rain.

I knew this rain could wash away my pain, and cleanse my battle stain.

I let the water wet my head, so I would no longer dream about the dead.

I allowed the water to wet my face, because I knew it would take my mind to a better place.

I stood until the water rose to my knee, to drown my PTSD.

The raindrops were cold, but I knew their healing power was more valuable than gold.

THEY NEVER TOLD US

They never told us how easy it was to die

They never told us how persistent and clever the enemy would be

They never told us this was the tour of a lifetime, and a lifetime tour

They never told us being home would feel so strange and awkward

They never told us how clearly we would remember the expressions on the faces of the dead and dying

They never told us we would remember the last words or conversation with those killed in combat

They never told us about the funny things that happen in war

They never told us how seriously wounded a man could be, and not have a scar

They never told us, one day, we may not be sure who we are

They never told us, they never told us, they never told us...

And we didn't think to ask.

LET THE LIGHT IN

Let the light in so your day can begin

Let the light in sunshine is your friend

Let the light in so that evil may not dwell within

Let the light in to kiss your face and caress your skin

Throw back the sash, draw the curtains, open the blinds

Let the light in, so your day can begin.

TELL ME YOUR STORY

Tell me your story from cover to cover,

from the first page to the last, let every chapter

detail your past. From shame to glory,

just tell me your story.

FALLING LEAVES

I catch the falling leaves out of the corner of my eye
before they hit the ground. Rarely does any movement
escape me now. See what war has done to me.

I'm always ready:

Ready to fight

Ready to run

Ready to shoot a gun

Ready to die

Ready to cry

Ready to be tense

Ready to use my sixth sense

Ready for defense

Ready for offense

Ready to detect falling leaves, before they hit the ground.

See what war has done to me.

I'M SO BLESSED

I'm so blessed, it looks like you picked me special over all the rest. And every day, I create a mess, doing things to put your grace and mercy to the test. But yet; I'm so blessed.

KEYS

I got keys, you got keys, we all got keys. In fact I've got a drawer full of keys. Old-fashioned keys, fancy modern keys, shiny new keys, old rusty keys, big fat keys, skinny little keys, electronic keys and keys of various degrees. Keys to the house, keys to the garage, keys to my car -- although sometimes I don't know where they are. Just recently I thought to myself, why do I have so many keys? But I don't have a single key to unlock this PTSD.

WINTER TRAIL

I glory in the solitude as I hike along the winter trail.
The sound of my boots compacting virgin snow,
leaving a deliberate deep waffle pattern to mark my
path.

Farther and farther away from the main road I march,
so that I cannot hear the sound of cars and trucks
coming and going along the plowed highway.

Now I can only hear my breathing synchronized with
my steps as a brief vapor of my warm breath quickly
dissipates into the crisp, but refreshing air, tingling my
throat and lungs as the frosty fresh oxygen rushes in.

I wonder how many partake of a stroll along the winter
trail. Viewing, admiring, analyzing and accepting God's
awesome beauty.

Free to all, who care to see.

A quiet stroll that sets my soul free.

Step-by-step, I blaze a trail of glee.

Peace, solitude, nature and me.

I CRY AT NIGHT

When the battle has taken a recess and I have a few moments alone, I cry at night. No one can see my tears at night. At daylight, I must show that I'm ready to fight. Only at night can I ask God why some lived, and some died, and cry at night.

MOVIE IN MY MIND

As I smile and talk casually with you about the weather,
there is a movie playing in my mind.

No well-known actors or movie stars appear in this
film,
just heroes.

This theater does not sell popcorn, there's no
intermission.
The theater has only one seat.

My movie is not approved for all audiences;
its raw footage does not have a rating.
It starts and stops automatically, but a picture, sound,
or certain smell and get the film rolling.

My movie has been playing for only a year, but some
have been at the theater more than 30 years. Many
before me and countless after me will develop, produce,
and star in their own movie.

THE PARK

Where are those parks, the ones we knew as kids. The park that some of us caught our first fish. And as the years passed, that same park may have been the same place we had our first summer kiss.

Those parks were so grand, there was so much to do and see, and explore. And when we had enough of fishin' or they just weren't biting, we could ditch our cheap K-Mart poles and go to the other side of the park and ride the bumper cars or try to win a stuffed animal playing skee ball.

We had fun at those parks, we could stay all day, and hated to go home. Sometimes, our parents planned an outing to the park in advance and the anticipation would kill us because we could hardly wait for the day. We would make an agenda how our day at the park would go. We tallied how many times we would ride our favorite ride, how many fish we're going to catch and how big, or how many hotdogs we were going to eat. Sometimes our parents would just announce out of the blue let's go to the park, and we would scurry to get ready, running out of the house to the car because our favorite park was not that far.

Those parks gave us so many fond memories us as children. The amusement section, the picnic areas, the trees, the grass, and those yellow and blue paddleboats you could rent at the boathouse.

Have you seen the neighborhood parks today, they surely aren't the same way. Today, only a fool would go to the average park after dark.

Not long ago, I visited my childhood park and I stood amazed how desolate and run down the park appeared to be. Groups of homeless men and women sitting around the park, drinking beverages from brown paper bags with their bicycles leaned against trees. The amusement section is gone, nothing in this area but poorly maintained grass and picnic benches. The little lakes that young anglers first learned to cast are now stagnant dirty bodies of water with trash and empty plastic bottles loitering at their banks. Wrought iron gates encircle the park now. Yellow barrier gates block off the access roads.

What happened to our neighborhood Parks? What happened to America?

FACES

All we have left is memories of faces, the war took away life without traces.

A mom hurt by a stupid war that took away her baby boy.

How much did we gain to justify her pain?

Just memories of faces lying still in unfamiliar places.

HAPPY VETERANS DAY

Today, I celebrate Veterans Day.

But it could've gone the other way,

then you would honor me on Memorial Day.

WHO CAN I CALL

I have phone numbers to several people who say call
me anytime, but it's 2 AM, courtesy and decency
wouldn't allow me to call past 9 PM.
Who can I call?

Nothing has worked out right in the past two days and
I have not slept twice that number of days.
Who can I call?

I'm battered by one of life's storms, the strong winds
howl and bend me at the waist as I try to stand or walk.
Who can I call?

Things seem worse, and this time, surely I think I will
fall.
Who can I call?

Is there anyone who will sit with me and sip hot tea.
Who can I call?

Can I call on those who rescued me from drowning in
the lake when I was 15?

Can I call on the one who let me walk away unscathed
from a serious automobile accident at 19?

Can I call on the one who watched over me in battle?

The storms rage within, I have no peace, and sleep
evades me.

Who can I call?

And when I call, what should I call you?

Should I call you my God?

Should I call you my Jesus?

Or should I simply call you my friend.

Who can I call?

THE POLITICIAN

I would have never known a war zone would have so much political appeal.

The zeal of our elected officials to meet and greet.

Hello son, what's your name and where you from?

Maybe they feel their weak hand shake and fake smile is a Warriors special treat.

Why are they here I would ask? Disrupting battles daily task.

Extra cleaning and sweeping, wounded hearts pretending not to be weeping, more cleaning and sweeping.

The chosen few, usually low in rank, rehearsing questions, but not really frank.

A special meal, something fancy like veal.

The entourage on their way, I mark my calendar and say, thank you Lord for another day.

PEACE IN WAR

What a contradiction of words. Who would ever think
or say there is peace in war.
Any grunt will not hesitate that he can relate. Yes, there
really is peace in war.
There is order.
There is structure.
Life is simple.
Your possessions are few.
There is peace in war.
My highly anticipated return home was met with
chaos, noise, disorder, and mass confusion. This is the
type of environment one would expect in war, and to
make it worse, no one seemed to be in charge.

My simple life was taken from me. No longer could I
exist on two pairs of boots, a few uniforms and my
prize possessions stuffed in a duffel bag or neatly
packed in a tuff box.

Every day I received phone calls, emails, and letters in
the mail, demanding my attention, demanding a
response, and yes, demanding money too.
The only thing demanded of me in war was to stay alert
and stay alive.

Yesterday my enemy was a speeding SUV bearing down on me on the freeway, last night was an unsolicited call from a telemarketer. Today, I cannot tell you who my enemy will be, what they will look like. But one thing I do know, there was peace in war. Engagements are loud, brief, and fatal. But then there was peace, because it was war.

NOT YOUR TIME

You could be a millionaire or only have one thin dime, there's nothing you can do if it's not your time. Everyone huddled around to lay words and eyes on me, assessing the situation and damage with awe and amazement, then locking their gaze on me as if I have committed a major crime. After a brief silence an anonymous voice from the background profoundly says, "Man, it ain't your time."

On the outside I'm unscathed, just a small scratch that hardly drew blood. Inside, My heart is racing, hand shaking, voice quaking.

Noticeably quiet for the next two days, my thoughts to myself, questioning everything about life, living, and death. But ultimately saying why him and not me, what if it had been me?
Maybe it's just not my time.

ON PATROL

I arrive at my destination without any major incidents.
There were two potential situations along the road. But
thanks to tactical vehicle training, I was able to avoid
danger. I shut down my vehicle and secured my
electronics. I scanned the area before stepping out of
my vehicle, failure to follow standard operating
procedures could mean the loss of a foot, leg, or your
life. My objective is located on the second floor of a
large commercial building in the southwest corner.
According to intelligence, the threat level is low, but I
know anything can happen anywhere.

I completed my mission in less than 15 minutes.
I'm back in my cruiser strapped in and ready to roll.
I purchased the needed dress shirts from JC Penney's.

But when will the mission be over in my head.
When will my mind allow my body to sleep through
the night.
When will I be given the "ALL CLEAR."
When can I stand down?
It's been a year now.
Why am I still on patrol?

WRITER'S BLOCK

What is going on in my head
that makes my pen go dead?
How I wish, I could go to bed.

What force so strong,
everything I scribble seems so wrong.
This I have pondered long.

Who will help me bind
that creature loitering in my mind
so that words and phrases I may find.

Thoughts and ideas so slow
there is no measurable flow
words simply say no.

Up the word stream
I row and row
swiftly pushed back by the currents flow.

Such topics I do know
yet my pen will not go.
Blank paper is all I have to show.

Through the still darkness I force my pen to write
pressing creativity to a new height
I will not succumb to this writer's plight.

With the breaking of dawn
new ideas begin to spawn
a sunny meadow warming a sapling and fawn.

Now I can say to you with great delight
things great and small that cross my sight
inspire me to take out my pen and write.

ABOUT THE BOOK

Greg Buffington is a military veteran who lives in Southern California. He served in Afghanistan from January 2007 to January 2008.

On October 4, 2007, his convoy struck an Improvised Explosive Device 16 miles south of Forward Operating Base Ghazni.

Pardon My Silence is his first book of poetry.